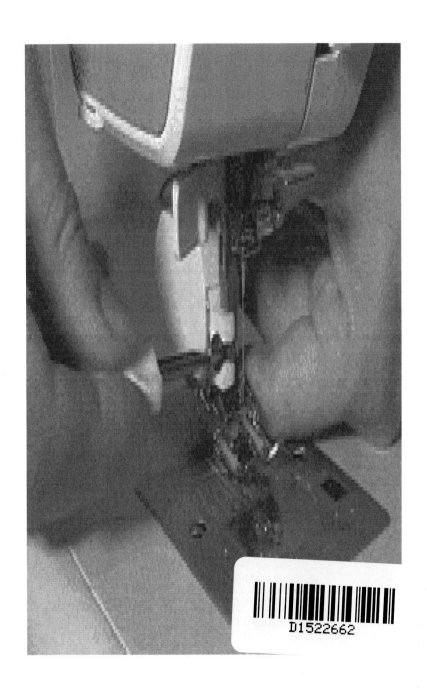

D1522662

WALKING FOOT QUILTING

Tips and tricks how to use walking foot for your quilting designs, Stitching lengths and other ideas.

Paulline Billy

TABLE OF CONTENTS

INTRODUCTION

I love the effects I get from straight lines as well as decorative stitches. (Yep, you could use some decorative stitches in connection with your walking foot to append texture as well as interest to your quilt.) If you have attempted to quilt using a frequent presser foot, you have observed that the upper fabric bunches as well as pulls, and the top layer is pushed uniformly on a foot while the feed dogs monitor the backing layer movement beneath it.

As a result, you will trim wondrously. Your foot has many choices from quilting straight lines to decorative stitching, plus curves.

In this book, we will discuss how you can set or install your walking foot quilting and various steps on how you can use a walking foot to quilt and a lot more.

PART 1: UNDERSTANDING WALKING FOOT QUILTING

The majority of sewing machines come with a feed foot also known as walking foot. Some machines have also an integrated feeding mechanism.

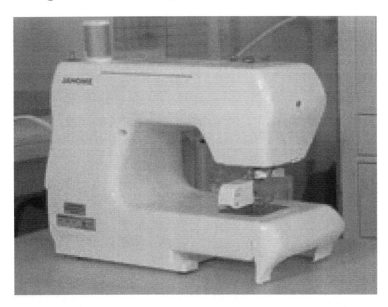

A walking foot will actually support your machine in an equal state to the wide quilted sandwich, and therefore you will not produce pucker as well as pleats as you quilt the top, bat, and back lay.

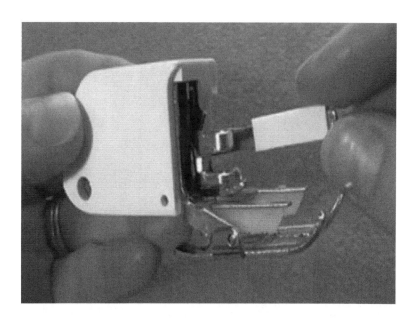

WALKING FOOT QUILTING:

Generally, the foot offers gripping gestures from the top or edge of the fabric that correlates with the grip of the feeding dogs that are installed in your sewing machine bed. As the lower feed dogs pull and perhaps feed the fabric under the needle to even make the stitches, the foot grips as well as pull the fabric from above.

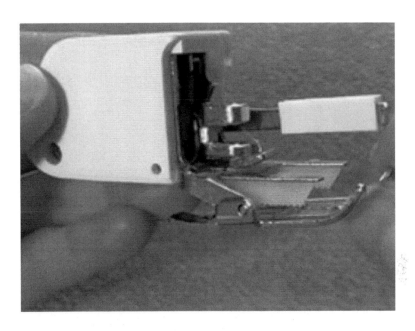

WALKING FOOT QUILTING – IS IT OPTIONAL?

Sometimes quilters ask me whether using walking foot is optional? My answer to this is yes! So, when is walking on foot optional?

There seems to be little walking foot need when you deal with two layers of a relatively strong woven fabric. Your feed dog's resistance against a normal foot offers all the friction that the fabric layers need to move smoothly.

WHEN WALKING FOOT IS NOT OPTIONAL

When quilting with oilcloth requires the use of a walking foot to hold "sticky" fabrics going.

It's challenging for the machine foot to apply suitable pressure to prevent the fabric layers from moving as you have multiple layers of fabric or thicker, canvas-type fabrics. The problem can be solved by regular pinning.

A walking foot makes all the layers of fabric including batting to running easily and steadily while quilting layers of fabric with batting. Whether you are making a bigger quilt or a little tote, this is essential

PART 2: DIFFERENCES BETWEEN QUILTING FOOT AND WALKING FOOT QUILTING.

While machine quilting, a walking foot comes in handy. The inner batting, fast batting, as well as bulky layers are sandwiched between three layers of fabric in a quilt. Unlike a normal presser, the walking foot can quickly move around as well as feed the quilt.

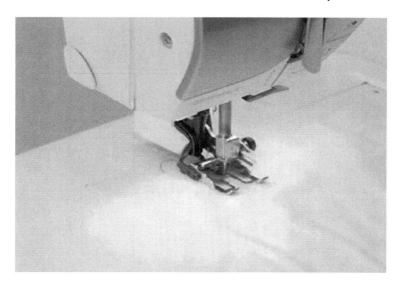

The followings are the major differences between quilting foot and walking foot quilting.

STRAIGHT LINE AND DIRECTIONS:

With quilting foot, it is possible for you to feed the fabric from either direction while the walking foot is only suitable for straight-line quilting due to its size.

ACCURACY LEVEL:

Walking foot increases the level of accuracy while also preventing the layers from slipping and quilting the foot On quilting designs, that creates a lovely textured effects.

COST:

Walking foot is costlier than other forms of presser feet while quilting foot is more economical.

MULTIPLE USES:

It's primarily used to stitch multilayered quilts that would be impossible to stitch using a standard presser machine while quilting foot is mostly used for embroidery as well as quilting.

PART 3: THINGS TO LOOK OUT FOR IN WALKING FOOT QUILT.

Each walking foot is fitted with a bar or fork that runs on the needle screw. The walking foot swings as the needle bar rises, as well as the feed dogs connect.

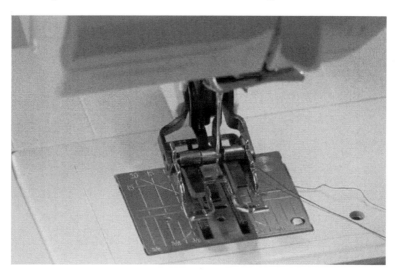

The bottom of a walking foot does have its feed dogs. This mechanism works in conjunction with the feed dogs on the sewing machine to carry the quilt sandwich layers into the machine equally.

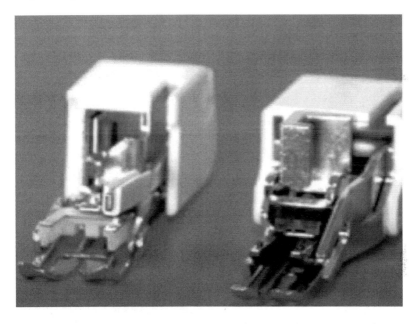

The followings are things you need to consider before purchasing:

OPEN TOE VERSION:

If necessary, buy an open-toe model. "Stitch in the ditch hole" Quilting is simpler if nothing would be between the eyes as well as the needle pierces the fabric and follows marked lines in a quilt pattern.

CONSIDER THE MANUFACTURAL:

When you buy your walking foot, consider your machine as well as the model of the machine. Footprints can differ within one company's line from model to model.

TYPE OF SHANK:

Know what kind of shank you have in your machine. You will buy a generic part if the maker no longer produces the model. To get a foot that suits correctly, you will have to consider the shank style.

GUIDE FIT:

This guide is put on the foot and gives parallel quilting lines a move. Only mark the first line and then let the rest of the foot do. There will be a channel guide to the left and right.

PART 4: HOW TO QUILT WITH WALKING FOOT

The simplest way of quilting is by using a walking foot. First, make a quilt sandwich to fit your quilt. Place the walking foot on the machine; the foot in the U-shape is a foot walk from the middle. You now have to configure the point as well as pick the running point. Ensure the stitch length, as well as width, are adjusted.

To get started, select the correct point on the quilt. A better approach is still beginning from the center. Start by cutting the quilt edge and stitching from one edge to the next. You can change the configuration of the machine continuously also the length and width to achieve further designs.

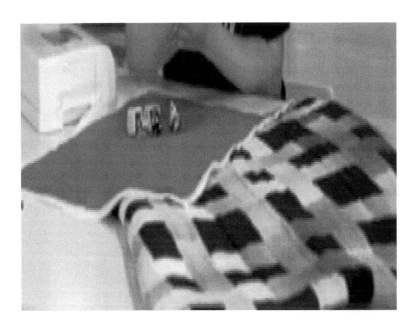

STEP-BY-STEP ON HOW TO QUILT WITH WALKING FOOT

Stitching is the toughest part after you have pieced the layers of fabrics. If you don't have the right walking foot, free motion quilting may get a tad more challenging. A walking foot will marvel in making the quilting effective if you are in a straight line.

The followings are how you can use a walking foot to create quilting but you need these materials for your proper quilting:

Walking foot	Quilting gloves	Batting
Painter tape	Cutting mat	Rotary cutter
Pieced quilt top	Spray baste	

STEP1: BASTING YOUR QUILT PROPERLY

If you begin to attach your quilt, it will help. Take a sandwich quilt on a smooth, wider surface. You should even tap your quilt from behind so it doesn't move. Make sure that there are no puckers between the fabrics, even on both directions. Take the pulverizer out of the edges while things are smooth Start to smooth out of the top. You should cut the tapes and iron to press the basting when the spray bottom is stable.

STEP 2: ATTACH THE FOOT

It's necessary to fix the foot on the machine. The bracelet is u-shaped and hits the right of the pinch arm. This foot glides over and falls between the needle.

This can be secured on the left side with a clip or a lever. Be sure your foot is fixed fully on the machine, and as you stitch this will not come off.

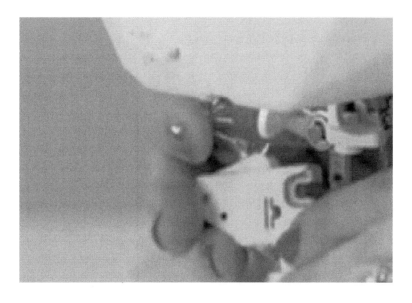

STEP 3: SET UP THE MACHINE

The next move is to launch the quilting process on your machine. You have to find the stitching after adding your foot.

An upright point for quilting is thought to be ideal. The length and width of the machine stitches can also be adjusted.

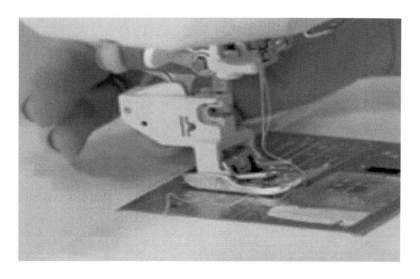

Make sure the length and width are selected according to the style of cutting you want to create. It must be noted that changes in the width of the stitches can affect the wave depth.

STEP 4: STITCHING PROCESS

You should not begin the stitching process until it is set up. If you chose the right position to start with, it will aid. When it comes to selecting the quilting side, everybody has a different choice. Center was always a favorite option to do something easily.

You don't have to see the bubbles or puckering if you begin from the center. Begin to stitch from the middle to hit the corners. When the opposite edge is reached, start stitching as well as cut the threads off.

You have to replicate the stitch with the current setup at regular intervals per block scale.

STEP 5: FINAL PROCESS

You should finish the stitching process until you have cut down to the preferred density. Square the surplus backing, thread, batting, binding, and so forth and trim. This is everything you would do to quilt with a walking foot.

PART 5: BACKSTITCH AND FREE MOTION WITH WALKING FOOT QUILTING

Some days ago some quilters ask me whether it is possible to backstitch with walking foot?

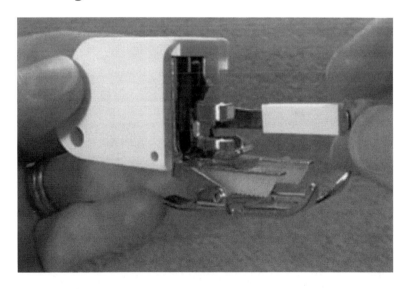

BACKSTITCH WITH WALKING FOOT:

Walking feet are flexible accessories with several points, but when it comes to backstitch it comes with a little bit of complexity. Walking foot is used for all kinds of forward stitching as well as back stitching it is something you have to backstitch. You can change it by adjusting the stitch height, but with a backstitch, you cannot use a foot completely.

FREE MOTION WITH WALK FOOT:

You need a walking foot for quilting because it will make sure that the stitches are uniformly spaced. The foot feeds uniformly into the quilt without leaving any irregular or unequal space.

Although when it comes to free motion quilting, you have to think a little bit about the smooth curves. A walking foot may not produce the smooth curves required for free motions

PART 6: WAVY LINE AND MATCHSTICK PATTERNS

If you are someone that likes straight line or curve patterns the stitch in the ditch is good in this aspect because those are the moves walking foot will do.

these designs give your quilt a visual boost, which will get others talking about your abilities.

These are easy designs that you did not know that walking foot could do:

WAVY LINE:

When it comes to quilting, novice quilters may believe that straight lines are the best bet. However, when you're just getting started, you should go for wavy lines. It is a wonderful way to get a feel on how to treat your quilt under a machine as well as there is less pressure   on   its   flawlessness.

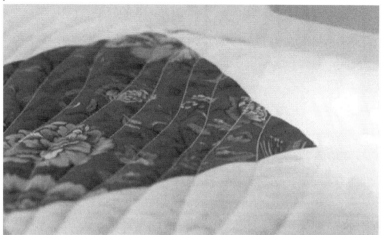

MATCHSTICKS:

Matchstick quilting is a process usually known as straight line quilting and it is mostly placed closely together like 1/8* or matchstick width apart.

This gesture can add more beauty to your quilting project when used with various colored threads.

PART 7: HOW TO USE WALKING FOOT

Multiple layers of fabric will move equivalently or uniformly into the machine with a walking foot. Stretch fabrics hems would pass straight under this foot not wobbly and stretching out, resulting in lumps as well as a puckered effect.

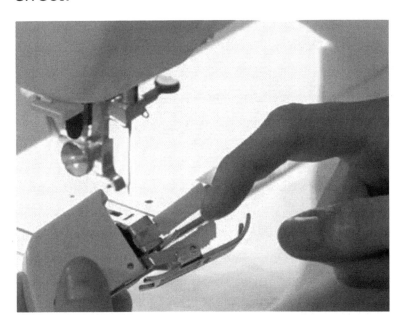

KNOW YOUR DIMENSIONS AND PARTS

The walking foot already has a constructed form of an in-built feed dog that functions similarly to the machine's feed dogs. The feed dogs on your machine are up to two to three (2 or 3) short and also thin metal bars in the side part needle plate of your stitching machine, mostly below your presser foot, that are crosscut with diagonal teeth.

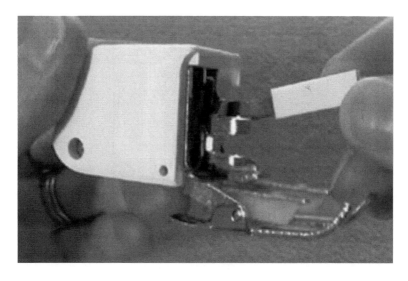

They march back as well as forth as you sew, dragging the fabric together under the presser foot. They march in accurately timed as well as calibrated intervals to establish the gap between each stitch. As the needle, as well as the needle bar of the system, goes up and down, the feed dogs of this foot begin to pace, pushing the presser foot trigger of the walking foot up and down as well.

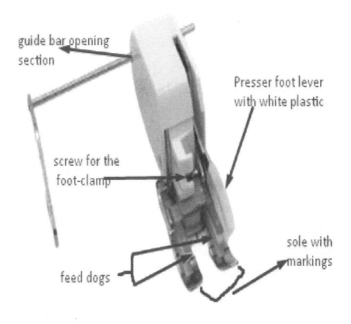

guide bar opening section

Presser foot lever with white plastic

screw for the foot-clamp

sole with markings

feed dogs

Opening toe walking foot consists:

A sole with an open toe including red seam as well as cornering marks that can be used as seam and cornering guides.

1. A short vertical line in the center marks the needle drop point (behind the needle). The ¼" distance from the needle drop point is shown by the other vertical points. For ⅛" distance, one of the metal tips of the sole may be used.

2. The horizontal marks for easy allow accurate corner pivoting, the red markings closest to the presser foot screw mark the needle drop point, and then you have markings at ⅛" and ¼". If you want ⅝" distance, you can just use the end of the sole as your guide.

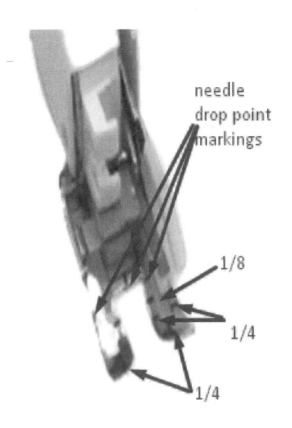

needle drop point markings

1/8

1/4

1/4

An arm with a plastic fork.	A right-hand arm with a white plastic 'fork' that rests along the needle bar (the presser foot lever) as well as where the needle fixing screw.
White plastic box.	The white plastic box comes with a small hole at the back used

	for attaching the guide bar.
Foot clamp	The presser bar holder, as well as the bar screw, uses the foot clamp to attach the foot.
2 rows of teeth	The two-row teeth stand ½ apart and they are the upper feed dogs

The foot comes with either a quilting bar or a guide as an option or you simply slip the bar into the white plastic box's back opening.

PART 8: HOW TO INSTALL FOOT ON YOUR MACHINE

In this part, we will discuss how you can install walking foot on your machine for use.

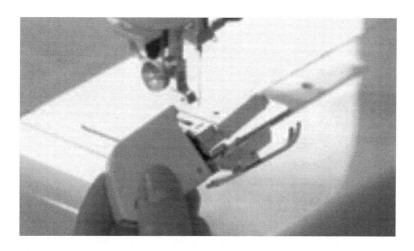

Firstly, it is necessary that you remove your presser foot as well as your machine's presser foot holder before installing your walking foot. Don't shift the needle to the topmost position because you will require the needle bar. However, not only the snap-on part that needs to be screwed off but the whole foot need to be screwed off.

When tightening the screw, slip the walking foot from behind as well as place the foot clamp along the presser foot holder screw on the left while still making sure the plastic fork stays around the needle bar on the right.

Move the needle up as well as down to see how it comes into contact with the sole's metal. The lever and the little fork around the needle bar should be rotating, and this is what controls or regulates the upper feed dogs, as you can see.

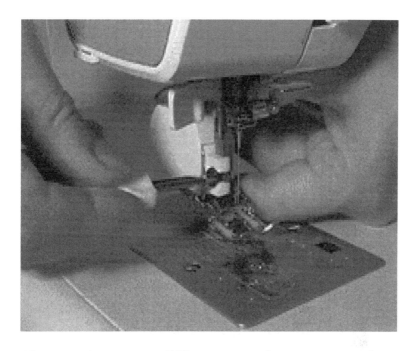

There is no difference between this machine and those with a low shank. However, you still need to disassemble the presser foot holder and replace it with the walking foot. You will still need a Bernina connector if you are using a Bernina.

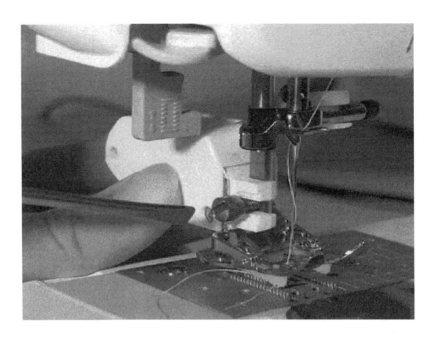

SEWING PROCEDURES AND INSTRUCTIONS

Most of the time, it is easy to sew with a walking foot you will need to stitch with a standard presser foot until it's allied. Sometimes, it is advisable not to be quick rather perform it at a moderate to slow level; this will lead to some level of accuracy. Some quilters use different kinds of stitches but in this aspect, you can use any of the stitches you want, even though you prefer to use a double-needle it can also function very well.

Using a special needle and possibly a zigzag stitch for knit and stretch fabrics. If the fabric is very frail, strengthen it with fusible interfacing before sewing the seams.

Since the top feed dogs will continue to move the top fabric forward, a walking foot should only be used for forward sewing. However, I have discovered that some walking foot can stand up 2-3 stitches backward while backstitching at the beginning of a seam.